# Become a Time Master

*How to Find the Hidden Time Opportunities in Your Day and Use Them to Maximize Your Productivity*

*Katelyn Silva*

# Get the Time Master Guide FREE!

## Read This First

Just to say thank you for buying my book, I want to offer you the Time Master Guide 100% free!

Go to:
https://write.theauthormentor.com/timemasterguide

# Table of Contents

# Introduction

Your shift is almost over for the day and you look at your watch, thinking of all the things still to be done when you get home. You think, "Okay, if I can just focus, I can get it done and still have a little time before bed." But then when you get there, everything is just overwhelming and you realize you're exhausted.

Before you know it, it's bed time, and you're wondering why you can never seem to make an actual dent in your to-do list. You feel like every time you do take a step forward, you take two steps back. The list just keeps growing no matter what you do.

If this is you, I have some good news and some bad news. The bad news is that this is life. There are always things that come up and things to be done. The good news is that you *can* get ahead and you *can* stop being overwhelmed. There is time for you! You just have to learn where it's hiding.

So how do you find this hidden time? Is it even possible?

I've never viewed myself as a master of time or organization. I've always felt that I could do better, do more. I never realized that in the process of trying to become more organized, others began to view me as exactly that. I've spent most of my life running full speed ahead without slowing down much. But that doesn't mean that I've missed out or failed to enjoy those special moments. I've just learned how to balance productivity with enjoyment.

Using these secrets, I have been able to write and publish multiple books, some under a pen name, and accomplish other projects, such as making crocheted items, while working full time as a restaurant manager and being a wife and a mom of two!

Over the course of my life, I feel that my experiences have really taught me what is most important and how to prioritize what needs to be done. For a long time, I didn't think I was organized or well-managed with my time. But then women began approaching me asking things like, "How do you do it?" That's when I realized that I had something to share and a way to help others. And ultimately, that's what I want to do.

So if you're feeling like you never have enough time in a day or are overwhelmed with everything in your life, sit back, take a deep breath, and remember: you can do this! And this book is here to help you find the time you're needing or think that you don't have.

As we go through the book, you'll notice a few little clocks and some notebooks scattered. I know, a little cliché! But they'll have next to them key tips or actionable points you can come back to and reference.

Just for you, I've developed a free guide book to accompany the book. In it are each of the actionable activities given throughout the book and plenty of space for you to take notes or do whatever you like!

You can get your guide here:
https://write.theauthormentor.com/timemasterguide

### Time-Master-Tip

- As you go through the book, pause and do each activity as it comes! This will help you start to implement the secrets and see change in your life.
- You can use the guide designed for this book, or you can get yourself a notebook or even use a document on your phone or computer. Whatever feels most comfortable for you!

Regardless of what you choose to use, I promise that if you do the actions, you will gain clarity and insight into your time and be able to get more done without packing on to the to-do list or feeling overwhelmed and stressed trying to get it all done.

# Mindset

*"Once your mindset changes, everything on the outside will change along with it."* – Steve Maraboli

I know, I know. Really? *Mindset?* Isn't everything out there nowadays about this?

Well, yes, and that's because it's so important. Mind over matter isn't just some abstract ideal or hocus pocus. If you can't organize and master your mind, how can you hope to do the same with your life?

Before you can master your time, you need to realize two things. Time management is about:

1. **Mindset and awareness, and**

2. **Organization**

As humans, we always do the things we feel are the most important. You're always going to have time to eat and sleep, as an example, because otherwise your body won't let you keep moving.

Take a moment and consider your day. What are the things you do every day without compromise? Is it time with family? Exercise?

Now consider the things you do regularly because they must be done such as grocery shopping, house-cleaning, etc.

Finally, consider the things that you do now and then or that you want to do more but always seem to get brushed aside because you 'don't have time'. What are they?

As you consider the things you want to do more, think about why you want to do them and why you aren't doing them now.

Why are these things important to you or why do you want them to be? What is really preventing you from doing them, other than 'time'? Is it fatigue? Other responsibilities? Lack of focus?

 *Action Guide Break*

❖ Use the guide and take some time right now to write out your current schedule, whether for the day or the week.

        o   If your schedule varies or is consistent, write it down. Be specific and detailed.

❖  Along with the exercise, include the things you considered and how much time you actually spend doing each task. Be honest with yourself, even for the small things like binge-watching Netflix before bed.

For an example, see mine on the next page. This is a recent one when I had gotten away from productivity and wanted to refocus my time and my life.

You'll see in mine that it's highly varied based on my day-to-day work schedule, but regardless of the fluctuation, there are every-day areas before or after my shifts where I was being unproductive.

| Time | Monday | Tuesday | Wednesday | Thursday | Friday | Saturday | Sunday |
|------|--------|---------|-----------|----------|--------|----------|--------|
| 7am | Get up, dressed, ready, etc. Kids up by 7:10 (prepare clothes, bag, backpacks, lunches, breakfast, etc.) | | | | | Same as week unless off or late shift. If so, up by 8:30, care for/time w/ kids | |
| 7:40 am | Be leaving house to take kids to schools. Drop off 1st by 7:45, next by 8 (if opening 10 mins earlier) | | | | | | |
| 8-8:30 am | Stop by store on way home for errands or groceries (gas, bills, etc.) after dropping off kids – if off or working later shift | | | | | Breakfast and family time if not opening ☺ | |
| 8:30 -9am | Breakfast for me and hubby – if off or later shift | | | | | | |
| 9-10am | House cleaning... if off or later shift | | | | | | Getting ready for church if off or later shift |
| 10-11:30am | Ambiguous, admittedly... spending too much time on games or Netflix (kids in school) – when I'm a mid | | | | | Time w/ family / church till I have to go in to work if not off | |
| 10-2pm | Same as above if not writing something, reading, doing more errands or cleaning... -- when closing | | | | | | |
| 5:30 - 7:30 pm | Time with family – reading, games, dinner, taking kids to park, etc. – when opening | | | | | | |
| 8:30 - 11:30pm | Ambiguous, admittedly wasting time with games, Facebook, Netflix, etc. (when open or mid) | | | | | | |
| Notes | Spending too much time when closing on watching shows or playing games. Need to refocus and form plan for time-spent | | | | | | |

- ❖ Once you've mapped out what your own day or week looks like currently, go back through and make note of your own areas of unproductivity or ambiguous times.
- ❖ Ask yourself:
  - ○ How much time am I actually spending scrolling through Facebook, watching Youtube videos or my favorite Netflix show, or something else?

In my example, I noted my areas of unproductive time when I made my schedule; I've used this method to reorganize myself many times. These notes will be used in just a moment!

Now that you've mapped out your current use of time, take a deep breath. We're going to take a moment for the fun stuff!

Step back and look at your future – the one you dream of. Let go and dream big. What do you want it to look like? What do you want your day to look like?

 Write down this schedule in the space provided in your guide, and again, be specific and detailed.

There's power in actually putting things down and out of your mind. It allows your subconscious to begin planning how this desire is going to manifest and become reality.

> *"It's only a dream until you write it down. Then it becomes a goal."*
> *– Emmitt Smith*

> *"Setting goals is the first step in turning the invisible into the visible." – Tony Robbins*

Before you can change anything, you have to be aware of your time and where it's going. All of the ambiguous places or "lost moments" I call '*time-opportunities*'.

## Time-Master-Tip

- o Those little notes we just made in our current schedule? They are moments in time where you could be more productive or could be doing something you really want to do to create your ideal future.
- o That is where your *hidden time* is. Those moments are where your magic is going to happen and where you'll be getting things done.

In my example, you saw that I have some pretty large time opportunities, at least when the kids are in school. But even if your time opportunities are only half an hour or less, they can still be huge areas for magic to happen!

If you're aware of your time, you can take control of it, and even get ahead of it. Let's dive in to how.

# Time Pacing

*"Lack of direction, not lack of time, is the problem. We all have twenty-four hour days."* – Zig Ziglar

As you look back through your notes of time opportunities, begin to consider your time-awareness as well. How aware of time are you during your day? How often does 'five minutes' turn into an hour and how often do you get to the end of your day wondering where the time went?

The next step to becoming a time master is learning how to budget your time, which begins as you gain awareness of how your time is passing and being spent.

For each thing that you do during your day, you can give yourself a budget of how much time you will spend on the tasks or activities. Whether it's getting the kids ready for the day or scrolling through Facebook, it can be budgeted.

## Time-Master-Tip

○ If you don't already wear one, I recommend getting a watch. It doesn't have to be expensive – but get something you like so that you'll *want* to use it. It's simple, but can be a powerful tool in mastering your time!

Of course, be realistic with yourself. Don't restrict the amount of time that real daily tasks actually take. If it takes an hour to get ready, be sure to give yourself all of that time. On the same note, do restrict things that are taking away from you. Sure, watch one episode of that awesome show. But if you have discipline, no matter how suspenseful that episode ends, you can always watch the next one tomorrow. The beauty of Netflix is that it will still be there, right?

If you're anything like me, you're a master of self-justification. "Well, I can just watch one more. It's okay. I'll double up now and make up for the lost time tomorrow." And this can easily become a cycle... until a week later you're wishing you had been a little more productive.

This is where accountability comes in.

Maybe for you, it's not Netflix. Regardless of what you spend your time on, if there are gaps where you're not doing something that will further your long term goals or that you would consider productive, it's a time opportunity, and at times self-motivation needs a little help.

In order to successfully make the necessary changes, it's so beneficial to have another person there, whether it's someone doing the journey with you, or just being there to hold you accountable, check in, ask questions, etc.

I highly recommend getting one such person on your side as you go through this journey. You're not alone in it!

One way to find an accountability partner is to find a Facebook group of people in a similar field or with similar goals to your own. If you're a writer, like me, my Facebook group is a great place to connect and share in a safe environment. Of course, it's totally optional. But whether you have an accountability partner – who can be a friend of yours, your spouse, or an associate – or not, being part of a wider, supportive group can help!

Whatever you decide to do, team up with someone else – and be a good partner yourself. Ask how they're doing, tell them about what you're doing, and set goals together so you can celebrate your achievements. Sometimes, just knowing someone else is there can help you get off that mental justification cycle and onto the action train.

Having this accountability will help keep you on track as you budget your time and give yourself limitations. Be intentional. Check Facebook but limit yourself. Maybe give five minutes out of your hour, or even out of your day. Get on, do whatever you got on to do, and get off. Otherwise, you'll lose more time than you intended to – which I'm sure you've had happen!

Budgeting your time helps with more than just time awareness. You'll no longer be wondering where the time went, looking at your clock at bedtime and wondering how your day got away from you again. Budgeting your time is the key to time management and getting ahead of time like I mentioned earlier.

When you budget your time, something else happens. You also become more *focused* with your time, because you know you only have a certain amount of time to get your current task done. You'll start to see that instead of looking at the clock, wondering where the time went, you'll be looking at it astounded at how much you got done!

 *Action Guide Break*

❖ Using your guide, make some notes about how you're going to budget your time.
❖ What things do you spend a lot of unproductive time doing that you could limit in order to maximize your time opportunities?
    ○ How can you also eliminate distractions, or at least reduce them in order to maximize your focus?

You can always come back and make changes! If you need some pointers, here is an example from my day:

My Time Gaps/Budgeting:

When opening – my time opportunity is after the kids go to bed until I go to bed, unless hubby and I are having time together. If he is working/studying, I could write, work on marketing or networking, or do something related between 8:30pm and 11pm. I could also limit myself to only 15 minutes of Facebook time for the day which I could do during my lunch at work, and can check emails between 8:30pm and 9:00pm. I could also use this time to get focused and relaxed before writing.

If I'm a mid – my time opportunity is from 9am-11am after kids are at school and house chores and errands are complete. I also have a time opportunity between 9:30pm-11pm (after work and kids are in bed).

In the morning, since it's harder for me to focus, I could check emails, take 15 minutes or less of Facebook time, and spend the rest of the time reading or working on marketing or networking. In the evening, after work, I can then focus and write before bed.

If I'm closing – my time opportunity is from 10am till 2:30pm after kids are at school and errands are completed and before I have to get ready to pick them up from school and head to work. I can most productively use this time by giving myself no more than 1 hour for emails, checking Facebook, writing any blog updates, etc. and then turning off all distractions and focusing on writing.

If it's a day off – my time opportunity is similar to the closing day and should be used accordingly. I can do laundry between 10am and 2pm (2 hours total) and also write while the clothes are washing and drying. Once the kids are in bed, that time on a day off is for time with hubby unless he is working or studying in which case it becomes a writing time opportunity until bed.

Note: if Saturday or Sunday, all time is spent with the kids unless it's between 1pm and 3pm for their nap time or after they're in bed.

Yours may be incredibly detailed, or an outline of the areas in your schedule you can use. The most important thing is that you create awareness of your time and the best way you can use it.

# Organization

*"He who every morning plans the transaction of the day and follows out that plan, carries a thread that will guide him through the maze of the most busy life. But where no plan is laid, where the disposal of time is surrendered merely to the chance of incidence, chaos will soon reign."* – Victor Hugo

Now that you have your schedule laid out before you, you know where your time-gaps are, and you're starting to budget your time, how do you start getting from your current schedule to your ideal one?

This chapter is all about exactly that.

The transition takes many steps. Like any journey, it's good to take one step at a time until you get enough momentum to start making the leaps and bounds. And you will. I believe in you!

I'm going to break it down into two overarching steps during this chapter.

1. **Goal Setting and**

2. **Day Planning**

Think about your ideal schedule as your long-term goal. Sometimes, these goals can be so daunting and overwhelming, right? But if you take your big goals and break them up into smaller ones – I'm talking so small you could accomplish one thing every day or every week, eventually, you'd achieve the big goal without even realizing how far you've come until you get there.

Wouldn't that be awesome? Wouldn't that feel so amazing?

That's what you're going to do. That's what the goal setting step is all about.

# Goal Setting

Go back to your schedule and your time gaps. Start thinking about the time that you're opening up by budgeting them.

What can you do with this newly found time?

Think of it in relation to the goal. What is one thing you can start doing now to make a long-lasting part of your life? Is it regularly exercising? Is it cooking a healthy meal? Or maybe it's learning to dance or paint!

Whatever it is, look at your current schedule and insert this new addition into one of the places you noted as a time-opportunity.

As that one thing becomes habit, go back through your schedule and note where you can add one more thing.

As each small goal is attained, work on the next one. Before you know it, you'll have achieved your big goal or your long-term ideal – without feeling like you climbed a mountain to get there.

While I've made this overview seem simple, the biggest thing that will make a difference is your taking action. Once you decide to add it to your life, do it! Share with your group, or at least with your accountability partner. Make the decision and then *make it happen.*

As you make one additional thing a habit, add something else to another time gap. This is how you start implementing small goals to reach the end goal.

The short-term goals are the ones you can take action and do *now* and the long-term goal is the one you can slowly work toward, piece by piece.

 *Action Guide Break*

❖ Take some time now and add your new habit or notes to your action guide. You can add it to the note section or your space for time opportunities and budgeting your time

This brings us to the next step. The best way to start implementing these new actions is by pre-planning your day.

# Day Planning

Even if you've never been a great planner, learning how to plan ahead will be not just beneficial, but key to your mastery of time.

Keep your planner or guide close by (if you're using a separate notebook), whether that be in your pocket, purse, or in your phone, and use it not only as a reminder, but as an encouragement. Start using it to pre-plan your day.

If you give yourself a written to-do for the day, you're more likely to do all of it. Why? Because when you have a plan, you can check your progress against it and it helps keep your mind focused and it prevents 'lost time'.

Plus, don't you love that feeling of accomplishment when you get it all done? Don't you love knowing that you did what you set out to do, even if it's small? I know I do!

Whether it's your day off or a long day at work, you can always plan how you're going to use your time. This ties back into time budgeting. Add the time you will spend throughout your day, whether it's errands, work, a phone call to a friend, or anything else.

Remember that for all the goals you have or things that you want to do, some of them are long-term and others are short-term. When you're planning, add in the short-term goals in order to get those feelings of accomplishment. The more that you do, the more you feel like you are able to do. There are small things you can do now to achieve your longer-term goals and that will allow you to make progress on a regular basis.

Again, be realistic and honest. This way, if you promised yourself you'd only spend an hour cleaning the house, and you keep getting distracted by the TV or emails, you can consciously realize your time is getting away and take action to make a difference instead of letting those distractions govern your time.

 *Action Guide Break*

❖ Use the area given in your guide to start pre-planning your days. This could be something you fill in on a daily basis, or something you pre-plan for your week or month, just depending on how detailed you want to be.

❖ Revise as needed to include new habits or celebrate accomplishments!

Even if you don't read the rest of this book, I promise that if you take the time to pre-plan your day, whether the night before or first thing in the morning, you will start to see progress.

But I want you to keep reading, because I want you to fully master your time so you can live with less stress and get more done. And it's not by trying to pack as much as possible into one day. That just leads to burnout.

Even with all the pre-planning and organization in the world, fatigue still happens. Mastery of time does not mean piling on as much as possible to 'get more done'. In fact, sometimes having less on your to-do list can mean actually doing more.

I know what you're thinking. How is this possible?

If you've never heard of the 80/20 rule, I highly recommend reading *80/20 Sales and Marketing* by Perry Marshall. While his book is specifically about marketing and business, it applies to all aspects of life. Essentially, 80% of your results come from 20% of your actions.

The idea is that you identify the one thing you can do to have the biggest impact. In some small sense, it's kind of like finding your individual butterfly effect for your life (of course, in a positive way).

The master of time has a full understanding of this rule and has learned how to apply it to their life. In order for you to become this person, you need to pace yourself, budget your time, and organize yourself.

There's one more thing that's part of maximizing your productivity and mastering your time: prioritization.

# Prioritization

*"The essence of self-discipline is to do the important thing rather than the urgent thing."* – Barry Werner

In the previous chapters, you really dove in to how you're actually spending your time and saw that there are places where you have time-opportunities. You also took a peek into your ideal future and wrote down what a day in your dream life would look like, and started taking steps to make that happen.

Sometimes, we think to ourselves, "Well, someday I'll..." Let me ask you something. When is *someday*? Exactly when do you want this to happen? How long do you realistically think getting there will take, and what actions need to happen to get there? If you don't know, or you've never thought about it, do this now!

For example, if you're tired of renting an apartment and you want to buy a house, use this section in your guide to write it down including all of the details. Where do you want the house to be? In your current town, or do you want to move? How big? What style? How expensive is it? Do some research and find out about mortgage rates in your desired neighborhood. Visualize it. Does it have a yard? A pool? A playground for the kids? What does this really look like?

Obviously, this is just an example, but take whatever your goal is and run with it. Whatever it is, ask yourself the questions and the details. If it's going to take $100,000, what can you do to start putting money towards it now? Can you cut that daily trip to McDonalds for breakfast out and instead cook at home? (Money adds up!) For the $100,000, if you can put away $300 a month by sacrificing current pleasures for later gratifications, you could make a really nice down payment for your house in just a few years!

What can you do to start putting a little away? And how long will it take you to save that money? Write it down, and make the goal concrete.

This book is not about how to achieve your dreams, but when you manage your time effectively, you'll start to see that attaining them becomes possible. It's good to give yourself goals and dreams. They give you something to work for and look forward to and they serve as a motivator to keep going even when you're tired or don't feel like it.

Sometimes those big dreams and goals feel daunting or overwhelming. I think that's why we put a 'someday' on it. It takes the pressure off of having to figure it out right this moment, among all the other things we have going on.

But did you know that making that decision and taking those actions can actually be very gratifying? It can light a fire that may have dimmed, or give us that feeling of accomplishment I talked about earlier. The best way to go about attaining a big goal is to break it down into smaller goals – small enough to be easily attainable every day.

Of course, there is a balance. I'm not asking you to just push aside your daily activities and responsibilities to go full throttle into all the other things you want to do. But that's where pre-planning comes in – and prioritization. In the last chapter, we talked about pre-planning your day and adding in one thing that you can start making a part of your schedule/routine. I also mentioned that one of these things can be a small goal toward your end goal.

How does this tie in to prioritization, then?

I'm talking about your desires vs. your responsibilities.

 *Action Guide Break*

❖ Use your guide and list out all of the things that you can't cut out or compromise on. Do you have a family? Or a job that demands a lot of your time?

- o (As a note, these things are your highest priority. They're the things you're going to spend time on no matter what.)
- ❖ Once you've listed the parts of your day or week that are highest priority, list out the other things that are not as important. What non-important things are you doing that you could give up? How important are your desires and long-term goals?
  - o Some of these things might be disguised as tasks you feel are necessary or productive, but are still taking time away from your long-term goals

Remember how I said we always have time for the things we think are important? In order for you to master your time and reach your goals, those goals have to become high priority to you.

As an example, writing is my passion. It's what I love to do and I can't imagine my life without it. In fact, if I go too long without writing something, I notice myself getting stressed. No, seriously! So take this into consideration. If you love photography, and you eventually want to do this full-time, how can you make it a part of your life and get serious about it? How can you prioritize making it into a business?

You'll always have time for the things that are the highest priority to you. That's why prioritization is so important as you're pre-planning your days. Without prioritization, you may get a lot done, but it may not be the things that would've advanced your goals. The things that really fulfill you. And you'll still be feeling overwhelmed, stressed, or even empty.

No matter what your life consists of, when you're able to do the things that matter the most or that 'light you up', those moments of fulfillment and joy give life a new meaning that can't be taken away. You'll go from feeling so many negative things like fatigue and frustration to feeling joy and an eagerness for the future.

It's similar to how being aware of world problems isn't enough – people have to take action to do something about it and see change. That applies to your time as well. You now have several tools to use to master your time and productivity.

Despite all of that, there are still going to be things that you can't do or that you need help with. How can you make sure that everything still gets done if this is the case? There are two more tricks I have to teach: delegation and time-breaks.

# Delegating

*"The way to get things done is not to mind who gets the credit for doing them."* – Benjamin Jowett

Sometimes a project is too big for one person, or you need help on your journey to reach your biggest goals. *That's okay.* It's okay to ask for help.

*The biggest mistake you can make while trying to master your time is to think that you can do it all yourself.* That's just not realistic and it's the quickest track to burnout. Thinking you have to do it all yourself will make you feel frustrated, stressed, and ultimately it will take you right back to where you started this book – overwhelmed and feeling like you just 'don't have enough time'.

That's not the result that I want for you!

There are some things you have to do because you really are the only person that can do it.

For example, only you can decide what you really want and what really makes you happy. But others can help you accomplish some of the actionable parts of the process.

I'll use myself as an example here. I'm a writer – but I don't try to do it *all* myself. It would just be too much. As productive as I seem to others, it's because I have a fantastic support system. A network of people that help me with every aspect of my books.

There is a group that reads the first drafts and helps refine it, as well as helping get the word out about it. I have an editor, a cover designer, and of course my husband and boys which are my motivating factor behind every book, every time.

Whatever your ultimate goal is or whatever you're trying to do with your time, you'd be surprised how many people will want to help and have skills and experiences that you need and that they can offer.

 *Time-Master-Tip*

o    Delegate things others have more expertise
      about or could work with you on so you can
      focus on the tasks no one but you can do
      ➤    This also helps free time for you so
            you're not stuck piling more on your list
            instead of getting more done!

The most important thing is that you let go of the illusion of control and let others give a little. I personally struggle with this sometimes. I always want to do more, be more, and help more. I struggle with feeling like I never do quite enough. There's always some way I could improve. This is great in that it allows me to constantly self-evaluate and get better. But the downside is that sometimes others feel like I don't let them in or that I don't trust them.

I've worked in restaurant management for a long time and a couple of years ago, I worked with a guy I was training to become a manager. His name was Jackson. We were very honest with each other in order to grow our careers and raise our performance. One day, I asked for his feedback. He asked me, "You really want to know?"

"Yes," I said, curious what he was about to say.

"You're really great at holding people to a high standard and doing your job. But you don't trust anyone. You need to let others do things to help. You can't do everything yourself."

Wow! That was kind of hard for me to swallow at the time. I didn't realize it until he pointed it out, but I really did try to do everything myself – because I didn't trust anyone else to do it as well as I could. Instead of letting them stumble, learn, improve, and eventually be able to do it as well as me, I just did it for them. That didn't help anyone.

That was the beginning of me really learning how to step back, coach others, and as a result allowing them to learn, develop, and feel like they were accomplishing something and doing well at their jobs. To this day, I will never forget that conversation because it was so very important to me. I'm grateful for Jackson and his honesty.

The same goes for you. If you struggle with trusting others or feeling like you have to do everything yourself, consider others' perspectives, or even your own history. You didn't start out doing it perfectly either. Someone along the way allowed you to learn and grow and they coached you how to get better.

Now it's your turn to offer that to the person who is following behind you. That person can then also feel like they are contributing something which will bring them joy.

So instead of feeling overwhelmed and stressed, delegate the tasks that, even if you can do them, someone else can and will too. Accept help from good people and it can only go well.

 *Action Guide Break*

❖ Use some of the space for notes in your guide to brainstorm or list the people in your life who you could delegate tasks for... or just ask for help!

> ❖ You could even reach out to people in your current network. You never know who might be connected to just the right person for your long-term goals!

Finally, the way you avoid stress and burnout while still accomplishing a lot is to take relaxation time and be gracious with yourself.

# Self-Grace

*"Never waste any time you can spend sleeping."* – Frank Knight

Despite your new-found productivity, there will be days when you just can't. For me, I've spent much of my life on the go-go-go, thousand-miles-per-hour marathon. However, that doesn't mean that I never take a break or don't know how to relax. Don't get me wrong, when I am relaxing, feelings of guilt from my lack of productivity creep in. But I've developed a saying for myself: "self-care comes first".

*How can I take care of anyone else if I'm not good to go myself?*

As the mother of three, a wife, working, and a writer on top of it, I know from experience that when I'm not 100%, I am not as good to the people around me that depend on me. I get grumpy, make excuses, and ultimately sell them short.

It's okay not to be completely productive with all of your time every single day. You'll get tired, get sick, or be dealing with sick children. During those times, it's important to give yourself some grace. I like to think of time as a coin. Yes, if spent poorly you can never get it back, but equally, when it's spent on something valuable, that can then be treasured forever.

Invest time with your loved ones and the things that matter. This is part of why we spent time writing down our high priority activities and responsibilities. I know my boys are at the top of my list. I would give up everything just for them – and they are also my driving motivation. The 'Why' behind everything that I do. So if that means that you sacrifice some of the time you'd like to spend on your goals to be with your loved ones, that time isn't wasted.

This also applies to yourself. If you need a sick day, take it. Relax, recoup, and watch Netflix all day. Whatever you want or need to get back to yourself – do it. But, just like with the things you limited and budgeted your time with, so it goes with relaxation as well.

Take time for yourself to avoid burnout, but also be aware of the time you take and don't let it get away from you. Take just what you need, and then hop back on the train. Again, it comes down to planning, organization, and prioritization.

There are plenty of days when I just need to take a nap while the kids are at school or even just take a twenty-minute bath after a long day to let my muscles unkink. I don't try to force myself to be productive when I know that I need some self-care time.

On the same token, I keep track of how much relaxation time I've had and refocus on productivity once I'm rested. At first, it can be like regaining momentum with a bit of a sluggish start, but through mindset and planning, I get going again in no time.

Ultimately, as you take control of your time, learning good balance is equally important. In the moments where you start to slink back to feeling like you're not doing enough, feeling overwhelmed, or like you just can't do it, consider your small successes and the feelings those successes bring. What is important to you and what are you already doing now that gives you joy? Playing with your kids? Or maybe traveling?

These are small wins that you can celebrate. Don't focus on what you're not doing, but instead *let the small things you are doing be your sense of accomplishment.* And then use them to motivate you to keep going and not give up or lose your ground!

# Conclusion

If you're one of those people that looks at others and thinks to yourself, "How do they do it?", just know that you can do everything they do.

I once heard something from a dear friend that my mom had told her before she passed away. She said, "Don't judge my insides by your outsides." What we see in someone else is only what they do and portray. We can't see their internal struggles, doubts, and fears unless they explicitly let us. And same goes for when others look at you. You see your own internal battles, but others don't. They only see the things you are doing.

So keep that in mind. Don't compare yourself to everyone around you. Focus on your own strengths and goals and what you can do to achieve them every day.

Go back through as many times as you want and review your schedule in your guide. Pre-plan daily and prioritize your to-do's. Do the things that are most important, and do something small every day for the longer-term goals that you want to accomplish. Delegate or ask for help on the things that you're really struggling to get done yourself or aren't quite sure how to achieve. And finally, have grace with yourself. You'll find that you're able to get so much more done when you're rested and at 100%.

I believe in you. *You can do this*. So believe in yourself!

> *"Believe in yourself, and the rest will fall into place. Have faith in your own abilities, work hard, and there is nothing you cannot accomplish." – Brad Henry*

# Master Your Productivity

I hope you found this book to be helpful and have gained some ways to really get more out of your day.

Before we part ways, I'd like to share something with you. If you've been reading time-management books, trying to get control of your life, and you still feel like you're on a roller coaster or a hamster wheel...

What you need is not how to manage your time, but rather how to take it to the next level and make the most of that time you're making.

I've created a step-by-step class where I give you applicable steps you can do to master your productivity. We all have the same 24 hours in a day, so why not learn how to accomplish the most out of each one?

Just hop over to this link:

http://write.theauthormentor.com/master-productivity

# More About the Author

Instead of the usual brief bio, I thought I'd take a moment, if you're interested, in sharing more about the course of my life and how I really learned the secrets of time management. It all started the day my mom passed away and I began to grow up.

I was eight years old and my mom had been struggling with breast cancer for several years. She called each of us – me and my five siblings – into her room separately. She was lying in her bed, her dark eyes bright and a smile on her face. "I love you," she said.

As I stood in my room after, I watched the hospital staff wheel her out of the house. I don't remember if it was later that day or the next day, but my dad came in and knelt in front of me and my younger siblings. "Mommy went to be in Heaven," he said. "She's home now."

At the time, I was too young to fully grasp it, and my siblings even more so. But that singular event was a pivotal moment in my life. After, we moved halfway across the country from Texas to Georgia, and started completely new. My Dad was never the same, focusing on trying to find a new 'mom' for us and providing. As a result, we felt left to ourselves. I first began shouldering more responsibilities when I was eleven, and it only progressed as I aged.

Through high school, I took on cleaning the house, doing the laundry, cooking dinner, waking my siblings, making lunches, getting everyone to the bus on time, and managing the bills and groceries, in addition to keeping my grades up and my other 'normal' kid activities I loved so much, like band practice.

At eighteen, I moved back to Texas and lived on my own working full-time as a single mom while attending college. Since then, I've married and had another son, moved again for my husband's nursing school, finished my first book, and gone on to publish two more.

Looking back, I feel those times of my life taught me many things including time management and productivity, specifically my life during high school as well as the last couple of years in which I've really returned my focus to writing.

I share this with you to say that regardless of what has happened or what life may throw at you, you can either let it be consuming and the excuse why you don't pursue your own future, or you can challenge it head on and pursue your desired life – no matter what!

# Other Books by Katelyn Silva

How to Rock Restaurant Management

Idea to Print: The Step-by-Step Guide to Kick Writer's Block's Butt and Finally Finish and Publish Your Book

Learn More at www.theauthormentor.com.

# Additional Resources

Become a Time Master Action Guide:

- Free eVersion:
  https://write.theauthormentor.com/timemasterguide
- Print Version:
  https://www.amazon.com/dp/1981232575

Become a Time Master Planner (so you can have an easy, practical tool throughout the year!)

- Print Version:
  https://www.amazon.com/dp/1099157722

Thank you so much for reading!

I hope you enjoyed the book and that you see great things start to open up and happen for you.

I would sincerely appreciate your feedback and anything you have to share. How can I make this book, and future books, better?

Will you leave a quick review on Amazon?

https://www.amazon.com/dp/B075FGPZST

Share your thoughts, even if it's just a sentence!

www.ingramcontent.com/pod-product-compliance
Lightning Source LLC
Chambersburg PA
CBHW030036230526
45472CB00002B/534

*9 7 8 1 9 8 1 2 0 4 3 2 8 *